THAILAND

BY MARY BATES

Essential Library
An Imprint of Abdo Publishing
abdobooks.com

ABDOBOOKS.COM
Published by Abdo Publishing, a division of ABDO, PO Box 398166, Minneapolis, Minnesota 55439.

Printed in China.
052025
092025

THIS BOOK CONTAINS RECYCLED MATERIALS

Cover Photo: Shutterstock Images (pagodas); SP Boongthong/Shutterstock Images (pattern)
Interior Photos: Shutterstock Images, 4–5, 6, 10, 16–17, 18 (globe), 22–23, 27, 34, 35, 40–41, 44, 54, 55, 59, 61, 64–65, 66, 72, 74–75, 76, 80–81, 82, 84, 88, 89, 92–93, 101; Lemaret Pierrick/Shutterstock Images, 9; Yongkiet Jitwattanatam/Shutterstock Images, 14–15; Red Line Editorial, 18 (map); Wanchana Phuangwan/Shutterstock Images, 24; Terry Whittaker/FLPA/Science Source, 28–29; Oriol Querol/Shutterstock Images, 33; Tristan Tan/Shutterstock Images, 37; Yaya Ernst/Shutterstock Images, 38; David Henley/Pictures From History/Universal Images Group/Getty Images, 43; Roland Neveu/Gamma-Rapho/Getty Images, 47; Pairoj/AFP/Getty Images, 48; Linh Pham/Getty Images News/Getty Images, 50; Chantal de Bruijne/Shutterstock Images, 52–53; Viacheslav Zhurbenko/Shutterstock Images, 60; Noraphat Vorakijroongroj/Shutterstock Images, 63; Kan Sangtong/Shutterstock Images, 71; Sanit Fuangnakhon/Shutterstock Images, 78; Anek Soowannaphoom/Shutterstock Images, 86–87; Louise Delmotte/Getty Images News/Getty Images, 95; Suchitra Poungkoson/Shutterstock Images, 98

Editor: Arnold Ringstad
Series Designer: Maggie Villaume

Library of Congress Control Number: 2024948603

PUBLISHER'S CATALOGING-IN-PUBLICATION DATA

Names: Bates, Mary, author.
Title: Thailand / by Mary Bates
Description: Minneapolis, Minnesota: Abdo Publishing, 2026 | Series: Essential library of countries | Includes online resources and index.
Identifiers: ISBN 9781098297046 (lib. bdg.) | ISBN 9798384919568 (ebook)
Subjects: LCSH: Geography--Juvenile literature. | Thailand--Civilization--Juvenile literature. | Asia--Juvenile literature. |Thailand--History--Juvenile literature.
Classification: DDC 915.93--dc23

CONTENTS

CHAPTER **ONE**

A TOUR OF THAILAND

As the plane prepares to land, Lily wakes up and eagerly looks out the window. Tall buildings reach into the sky. Lily and her parents left the United States yesterday afternoon. Now, after nearly 24 hours of travel, they are about to touch down at the airport in Bangkok.

Bangkok is the bustling capital city of Thailand, the second-largest country in Southeast Asia. Back in Los Angeles, it is ten o'clock in the morning. Here in Thailand, there is a dark midnight sky above. But from the plane, Lily sees a city alive with lights and activity.

The family exits Bangkok's Suvarnabhumi Airport, Thailand's main international airport. They are greeted with warm, tropical air. Colorful taxis line the street,

Bangkok is by far Thailand's largest city in both area and population.

Thailand's floating markets are popular among locals and tourists alike.

waiting for passengers. The travelers board one, and the taxi begins navigating the crowded streets of Bangkok.

Bangkok is home to more than 13 percent of Thailand's total population.[1]

Lily watches brightly painted *tuk-tuks* whiz in and out of the lanes around her, their engines making a distinctive "tuk-tuk-tuk" noise. They are just as colorful as the taxis, but their smaller size makes them nimbler on the congested streets. Lily thinks they look like a fun and fast way to get around the city.

Soon Lily and her parents reach their hotel, which is located along the Chao Phraya River. They carry their suitcases inside and get ready to rest. Lily is exhausted from the long day of travel. But she is eager to explore Thailand tomorrow.

SHOPPING AT A FLOATING MARKET

Lily plans to start her first full day in Thailand at one of the country's famous floating markets. At these markets, people buy food and souvenirs from vendors in long wooden boats. Historically, Thailand's waterways were its main mode of transportation and trade. Today, floating markets are popular tourist attractions.

Lily and her family travel to Taling Chan, a floating market located a few miles outside of downtown Bangkok. They take the BTS Skytrain, part of the city's public transportation system. At the market entrance, Lily notices the abundance of plants and flowers for sale. The smell of fried fish fills the air. Ahead, she sees a narrow river crammed with long-tail boats. They line the riverbank, tethered to floating docks. Many of the vendors are cooking and serving seafood. Others have an impressive variety of fresh fruits.

Lily points to a large, spiky fruit that she's never seen before. Her parents tell her it is a durian. Using a large knife and his hands, the fruit vendor opens the yellow durian. He scoops out some of the soft, pale pulp and offers it to Lily. It looks almost like vanilla pudding, but the smell shocks her. It reminds Lily of rotting onion. Her parents laugh and say it smells sweet to them. They accept the samples of durian. Lily takes a bite and is surprised that the fruit tastes like almonds.

EXPLORING A LOST CITY

After leaving Taling Chan, the family takes an hour-long taxi ride to the historic ruins of Ayutthaya. Founded in 1350 CE, Ayutthaya was the capital of the state of the same name. The city was powerful until a Burmese army attacked it in 1767. Ayutthaya was ransacked and abandoned. The ruins of the former city are now preserved as the Ayutthaya Historical Park.

Lily and her parents rent bicycles outside of the park to explore the ruins. They take breaks from

VENICE OF THE EAST

For centuries, the Thai people have depended on the Chao Phraya River and its system of small canals, known as *khlongs*. Before the 1900s, these waterways were essential for daily life. People used khlongs to travel and to transport goods. Khlongs were also used for irrigation, fishing, and sewage disposal. Bangkok was nicknamed the Venice of the East for its network of rivers and canals. Today, some khlongs have been filled in and turned into roads, though many are still waterways.

The ruins of Ayutthaya sit alongside modern buildings in the city of the same name.

pedaling to look up at the tall towers, called prangs, rising from the remains of ancient temples. Lily is stunned by the massive size and splendor of the buildings. The family passes other tourists, as well as Buddhist monks in their robes.

They slow down to admire painted murals on the crumbling walls of a former courtyard. Lily turns to see a stone Buddha head seemingly emerging from between the roots of a large tree. The remains of this Buddha statue became entwined in the tree's roots as it grew long ago, and now they appear fused together. Although the evidence of ruin is everywhere, Lily can easily imagine how glorious Ayutthaya must have been hundreds of years ago.

ABOUT BUDDHISM

The religion of Buddhism was founded approximately 2,500 years ago in India. Buddhists believe that by following the teachings of Siddhartha Gautama, known as the Buddha, one can achieve a state of enlightenment. In Thailand and its neighboring countries, most people follow a school of Buddhism called Theravada. Theravada means "the way of the elders," reflecting the belief that this form of Buddhism has remained closest to the original teachings of the Buddha. Theravada Buddhism emphasizes meditation to reach the ultimate goal of enlightenment.

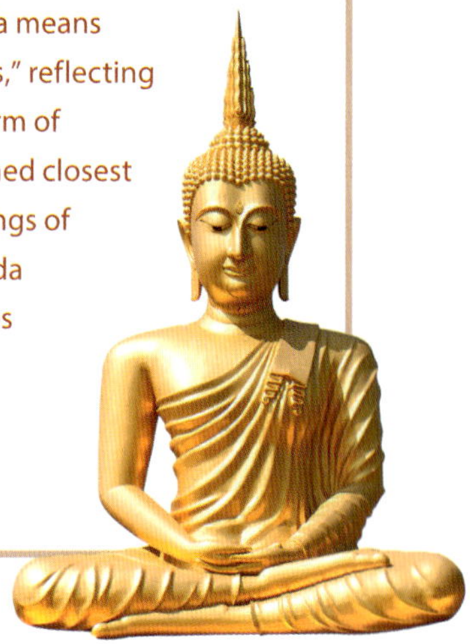

THE GRAND PALACE AND TEMPLES

In the afternoon, Lily and her parents head back to Bangkok. Even though the temperature climbs above 80 degrees Fahrenheit (27°C), they are all wearing pants and long sleeves. Their next stops are holy sites that require guests to cover their knees and shoulders.

At the Grand Palace, they begin to learn more about two forces that have shaped Thai life for centuries: the religion of Buddhism and the monarchy. The Grand Palace is a sprawling complex of more than 100 palaces, reception halls, temples, and courtyards in the heart of Bangkok.[2] King Rama I had it built in 1782 when he founded Bangkok as the capital of Ayutthaya, which later became Thailand. The Grand Palace was the official residence of the Thai royal family for generations. Today, the complex is used to host royal ceremonies and welcome foreign dignitaries.

In 2022 there were more than 43,000 Buddhist temples, or wats, in Thailand.[5]

As Lily strolls the grounds, she marvels at the ornate pagodas and glittering mosaics. But she is most interested in seeing the Emerald Buddha, Thailand's most sacred religious artifact. Lily read about it before her trip. The artifact is housed in the Buddhist temple Wat Phra Kaew, which is located next to the Grand Palace. Inside the temple, the atmosphere is quiet and calm. The 26-inch (66 cm) statue of the Buddha sits inside a glass box atop a throne.[3] It is not actually made of emerald. Instead, it is carved from a green mineral called jasper. The carving was done sometime around the 1400s. Lily admires the artistry of the carving as well as the Buddha's decorative gold and diamond crown.

Next, the family crosses the street to visit Thailand's largest Buddhist temple, Wat Pho. It is home to an enormous reclining Buddha sculpture. At 150 feet (46 m) long, the sculpture takes up nearly the entire building.[4] The sculpture is completely covered with gold leaf and contains intricate mother-of-pearl inlays on its eyes and the soles of its feet. Wat Pho houses more than 1,000 sculptures and images of the Buddha, making it the largest Buddha collection in Thailand.[6] Lily's family spends a few hours wandering the tiled courtyards and exploring the lavish chapels.

THAI STREET FOOD AND A RIVERBOAT RIDE

When Lily and her parents leave the temple, they are happy to see the streets lined with the stalls and carts of food vendors. The smells of lemongrass, chili, and garlic thicken the air, and Lily's stomach rumbles in response. She is eager to try some of Thailand's famous street food. Many stalls have menus with pictures of the options, which include stir-fries, noodle dishes, and curries with jasmine rice.

Thai cuisine often involves mixtures of differing flavors, such as sweet and savory or sweet and spicy. Lily chooses massaman curry, a coconut curry with savory ingredients. Still learning Thai, she orders by pointing to the corresponding picture. Her parents speak in Thai to order a noodle dish called *pad see ew*, dumplings, and *som tam*, a salad made with grated papaya, string beans, chilies, and spices.

As the sun sets, Lily's family hops on the Chao Phraya Express Boat to return to their hotel. This public riverboat is one of many boats in the water. From smaller long-tail boats to larger cruise ships and rice barges, the river teems with vessels.

Despite the noise and commotion of the busy waterway, Lily is relaxed as she studies her surroundings. The setting sun reflects in the water, along with temples, palaces, skyscrapers, and luxury hotels. The scenic view is a perfect illustration of how tradition and modernity are both embraced in Thailand.

As the boat nears the hotel, Lily and her parents talk about their day. All three agree that they could spend their entire trip in Bangkok and never get bored. But Lily knows there is much more to Thailand than its capital city. Tomorrow, her family will spend a day hiking and looking for wildlife in the forests of Khao Yai National Park. Lily hopes to see Asian elephants, the national animal of Thailand. Then the travelers will head south to the island of Ko Samui. The island offers beaches, waterfalls, and plenty of opportunities for snorkeling. Lily will be sad to leave Bangkok, but she is eager to explore more of Thailand's vibrant culture and natural beauty.

BANGKOK'S FULL NAME

In the Thai language, Bangkok is known as Krung Thep Maha Nakhon. This means "Great City of Angels." In everyday conversation, most Thai people shorten this to Krung Thep.

The capital's full ceremonial name is Krungthepmahanakhon Amonrattanakosin Mahintharayutthaya Mahadilokphop Noppharatratchathaniburirom Udomratchaniwetmahasathan Amonphimanawatansathit Sakkathattiyawitsanukamprasit. This translates to "City of angels, great city of immortals, magnificent city of the nine gems, seat of the king, city of royal palaces, home of gods incarnate, erected by Vishvakarman at Indra's behest." At 169 letters, the capital holds the world's record for the longest place name.

BANGKOK AND BEYOND

Thailand's cities are known for their cultural and historical attractions. But the country is also home to an impressive amount of natural wonder and biodiversity. Thailand is a land of varied landscapes,

Thailand's scenic vistas make it a popular destination for tourists from around the globe.

including forested mountains and hills in the north, rice paddies in the central plains, and a long southern coastline.

Today, Thailand is a major tourist destination. In 2023, the country welcomed more than 28 million visitors.[7] They come to explore Thailand's rich cultural heritage, history, and tropical landscapes. However, what truly sets the country apart is its people. Thailand's reputation for friendliness and hospitality has earned it the nickname the Land of Smiles.

CHAPTER **TWO**

GEOGRAPHY

Thailand sits just north of the equator in the center of Southeast Asia. It has a total area of 198,117 square miles (513,120 sq km).[1] This makes it around three-quarters the size of Texas. Thailand is the fiftieth-largest country in the world. It is a bit bigger than Spain and somewhat smaller than France.

Geographically, the country can be divided into two major areas: a larger section in the north and a narrow strip of land in the south. Thailand's irregular shape is sometimes said to resemble the head of an elephant. The northern part of the country makes up the animal's face and ears. The southern isthmus represents its trunk.

Thailand borders four other countries and two major bodies of water. The larger northern portion

Thailand has lush landscapes along its Mekong River border with Laos.

MAP OF THAILAND

KEY:

Capital

City

Point of Interest

of Thailand is bordered by Myanmar to the west, Laos to the north and east, and Cambodia to the southeast. Southern Thailand extends along the Malay Peninsula and borders Malaysia to the south. The Gulf of Thailand, which is part of the South China Sea, makes up the southeastern border. The Andaman Sea lies to the west. In total, Thailand's coastlines measure about 2,000 miles (3,200 km).[2]

THE GOLDEN TRIANGLE

In northern Thailand, there is a point at which Myanmar, Laos, and Thailand meet. It is called the Golden Triangle. This is where the Mekong River, the border between Thailand and Laos, joins the Ruak River, the border between Thailand and Myanmar.

This region has long been a hot spot of illegal activity, particularly the cultivation and trafficking of opium. However, the Thai side has become a tourist attraction. It is known as Sop Ruak. Visitors can explore souvenir shops, the Golden Triangle Park, and a museum dedicated to the history of the opium trade.

Thailand depends on two principal river systems. In the east, the Mekong River forms much of the border between Thailand and Laos. The Mekong River is the longest river in Southeast Asia, running about 2,700 miles (4,350 km).[3] It flows from China through Myanmar, Laos, Thailand, Cambodia, and Vietnam. The river empties into the Mekong Delta, southeast of Thailand.

The other major river system is the Chao Phraya River in central Thailand. Three rivers, the Ping, the Yom, and the Nan, flow south from the northern mountains. They merge to form the Chao Phraya, which continues south for more than 225 miles (362 km) before emptying into the Gulf of Thailand south of Bangkok.[4] Together, the Chao Phraya and Mekong systems support diverse vegetation and agriculture in Thailand.

LAND USE

Forested areas account for about 32 percent of the country's land.[5] Most of Thailand's forests are within designated protected areas, such as national parks, wildlife sanctuaries, or nonhunting areas. Despite some environmental protections, the area of Thailand covered by forests has decreased significantly during the past several decades. Some of the factors contributing to the loss of forest cover have included population growth, infrastructure development, agricultural expansion, illegal logging, and uncontrolled forest fires. At the same time, the amount of land covered by hard surfaces, such as roads and rooftops, has increased.

Thailand was once primarily an agricultural country. However, it has been undergoing rapid urbanization since the 1960s. Nearly 54 percent of the country's 70 million people now live in urban areas.[6] That figure is expected to grow to 72 percent by 2050.[7]

Bangkok is by far Thailand's most populous urban center. The Thai capital is also the fifth-largest city in East Asia in area, and it is the region's ninth-largest city in terms of population.[8] Other major cities in Thailand include Chiang

DEFORESTATION AND THE LOGGING BAN

In 1989, Thailand passed a nationwide ban on logging. The decision was made in response to devastating floods that were worsened by the effects of logging. It also became clear that the rate of deforestation was not sustainable. Despite the ban, forest cover continued to shrink, reaching 25 percent in 1999. Since 2000, however, the rate of deforestation has decreased. This is partly because law enforcement has become stricter. Today, forest cover in Thailand has stabilized at approximately 32 percent of the land.[9]

Mai in the mountainous northern region, Udon Thani in the flatter northeast, and Hat Yai in the coastal south.

THAILAND'S REGIONS

The varied landscapes of Thailand divide the country into four unique regions. The northern region is mountainous and forested. The central region, home to Bangkok, is a fertile river valley. The northeastern region consists of a dry plateau. Finally, the southern region on the Malay Peninsula has sandy beaches.

Northern Thailand is home to the Thai highlands, a mountainous region with lush forests and steep river valleys. The tail end of the Himalayas runs along Thailand's western border with Myanmar and down to Malaysia. Mountain peaks here average about 5,200 feet (1,600 m) above sea level.[10] The country's highest point is Doi Inthanon, at 8,415 feet (2,565 m) above sea level.[11] Sometimes called the roof of Thailand, Doi Inthanon is in northwestern Thailand, near the city of Chiang Mai.

Many rivers originate in northern Thailand, including those that form the Chao Phraya. Over time, these rivers carved deep valleys between the mountains. The fertile soil and cooler temperatures in these valleys support agriculture, including the growing of lychees and strawberries.

The Central Plains region of Thailand's interior is dominated by the Chao Phraya River basin. It is the most densely populated region in the country. It is also the political, economic, and cultural center of Thailand. The region consists of rolling plains that give way to the floodplain and delta of the Chao Phraya River. The land is low and flat. At the Gulf of Thailand, the elevation dips to sea level. It is the country's lowest point.

The fertile valleys of the Central Plains are important for agriculture, especially the cultivation of rice. Thailand is among the world's largest exporters of rice. Nearly half of the agricultural land in the country is devoted to rice production.

Northeastern Thailand consists of the Khorat Plateau. It is bordered by the Mekong River to the north and east. Mountains surround it to the west and south. The Khorat Plateau occupies 60,000 square miles (155,000 sq km) and sits 300 to 650 feet (90–200 m) above sea level.[12] It is dry compared with the more fertile areas of Thailand. However, flooding can occur during the rainy season. Like the Chao Phraya basin, the Khorat Plateau is a major rice-producing area.

Southern Thailand is a narrow strip of land on the Malay Peninsula. A mountain range runs down the center of the peninsula, with sandy beaches on either side. Southern Thailand also includes about 1,430 offshore islands.[13] Many of the islands are popular tourist destinations due to their scenic tropical beaches and warm turquoise waters.

Rice is grown in submerged fields known as paddies.

The Gulf of Thailand is a busy waterway for boats of all kinds.

ANG THONG NATIONAL MARINE PARK

Located in the Gulf of Thailand, Ang Thong was designated a national marine park in 1980. It includes 42 small islands spread over 39 square miles (102 sq km).[15] Only two of the islands are inhabited. The landscapes include rocky limestone cliffs, inland marine lakes, caves, rock formations, mangrove forests, and sandy beaches. Researchers have documented more than 50 species of birds, 16 species of mammals, 14 reptile species, and five amphibian species within the park.[16]

People enjoy sailing, kayaking, diving, snorkeling, and much more in these beautiful waters. The largest of Thailand's islands are Phuket in the Andaman Sea and Koh Samui in the Gulf of Thailand. The nation's southern coastal areas and islands feature beaches, forests, waterfalls, coral reefs, and mangrove swamps. In addition to tourism, the region supports the fishing and agriculture industries. There are many rubber plantations and fruit orchards found in this part of the country.

CLIMATE

Thailand's climate is influenced by its location within the tropical monsoon zone of Southeast Asia. It is relatively hot and humid throughout the year. Temperatures typically range between 66 and 100 degrees Fahrenheit (19–38°C).[14] However, areas of higher elevation in the north can occasionally experience frost.

Thailand's tropical monsoon climate is characterized by a seasonal reversal of winds. This results in distinct wet and dry periods. Most of the country, except for the southern isthmus, experiences three seasons. The seasons differ in precipitation, temperature, and humidity.

The rainy season spans from May to October, with precipitation peaking around September. The average yearly rainfall in Thailand is 56 inches (142 cm).[17] Most precipitation occurs during the rainy season. The amount of rainfall varies somewhat between regions and with altitude. But rainy season floods can be frequent, even in major cities.

Starting in November, the prevailing winds change direction. This results in cooler, drier weather through February. This is the cool season, marked by milder temperatures, little rainfall, and less humidity.

During March and April, Thailand experiences a short, hot period. The air tends to be still and dry during this time. Temperatures in Bangkok can soar above 100 degrees Fahrenheit (38°C).[18]

The climate in southern Thailand is moderated by its proximity to the sea on both sides. This region experiences a shorter dry season. Southern Thailand is more consistently hot and humid. Temperatures average around 85 degrees Fahrenheit (29°C) throughout the year.[19]

Between 1953 and 2023, the average annual temperature in Thailand increased by 2.3 degrees Fahrenheit (1.3°C).[20]

Southern Thailand's coastlines and islands experience a more moderate, comfortable climate than the northern part of the country.

CHAPTER **THREE**

PLANTS AND ANIMALS

Because Thailand has a range of climates and geological zones, it also has an impressive amount of biodiversity. The country has a variety of habitats across its forests, freshwater areas, and marine environments. These habitats support diverse plants and animals.

Thailand lies within the Indo-Burma biodiversity hotspot. This is one of 36 areas on Earth recognized for being biologically rich and threatened.[1] Thailand has approximately 15,000 plant species, 300 mammal species, 980 bird species, 320 reptile species, and 120 amphibian species. Its waters are home to about 11,900 marine invertebrate species, 2,100 marine fish species, and 700 freshwater fish species.[2]

Indo-Chinese tigers are found in only a few Southeast Asian countries, including Thailand.

Thailand is home to 8 percent of the world's plant species.[4]

The historical exploitation of natural resources has threatened this biodiversity. Thailand's endangered species include large mammals such as Asian elephants and Indo-Chinese tigers as well as marine species such as hammerhead sharks and sea turtles. Thailand is one of only five places in the world where the Irrawaddy dolphin lives. It is estimated that fewer than 20 of these freshwater dolphins are left in Thailand's waters.[3] The country is also home to many endangered plants. These include orchids and carnivorous pitcher plants.

Some threats faced by Thailand's wildlife are caused by the growing human population. Infrastructure growth and urban development have crowded out many wild habitats. Despite a 1989 logging ban, Thailand's forests are still vulnerable to threats such as illegal timber harvesting, uncontrolled fires, and agricultural expansion. Poaching and the illegal trade in wild plants and animals are also serious problems. For example, Thailand is one of the top countries involved in the illegal trade of pangolins. These small, scaled mammals are highly endangered and are considered the world's most trafficked mammals.

Other threats facing wildlife include air and water pollution, especially around major cities such as Bangkok. Plant and animal species in Thailand are also vulnerable to climate change. A warming planet is worsening extreme weather events such as tropical storms, floods, and droughts. The Global Climate Risk Index, an annual report published by a German environmental organization, ranked Thailand among the world's top ten countries most at risk due to climate change.

ELEPHANTS: THE THAI NATIONAL ANIMAL

Elephants have played a vital role in Thai society for centuries. They helped shape the country's history and culture. Today, the elephant remains an important national symbol.

In Thailand, elephants are associated with royalty. The animals represent strength, wisdom, and good fortune. They also hold a deep spiritual significance because of their associations with the religions of Buddhism and Hinduism. The spiritual and symbolic importance of elephants is seen in Thai belief systems, art, and literature.

Historically, elephants served practical and ceremonial purposes. Elephants were used in wars to carry troops and intimidate the enemy. They played important roles in royal parades, demonstrating a king's power. Elephants were also a big part of Thailand's economy, especially its logging industry. They were used as working animals to help with heavy labor and transportation. Elephants can navigate dense jungles and carry heavy logs, which made them ideal for timber extraction.

However, the role of elephants in Thailand changed in the late 1900s. As Thailand became more

THAILAND'S TIGERS

Years of conservation efforts may be improving life for Thailand's tigers. A 2024 estimate put the number of wild tigers in Thailand somewhere between 179 and 223. That's up from as few as 148 tigers in 2022.[5] Thailand is the first country in Southeast Asia to increase its wild tiger population.

Thailand's Western Forest Complex is the biggest forested area in the country. This forest supports the largest single population of tigers left in mainland Southeast Asia. Between 2007 and 2023, this tiger population is believed to have increased from 41 tigers to 143.[6]

industrialized, machines replaced elephants in industries such as logging and agriculture. And in 1989, the country banned nearly all the logging that had employed elephants.

Thailand's elephants found new work in the country's growing tourism industry. Today, tourists can seek out a variety of elephant experiences. These range from observing and feeding the animals to bathing or riding on them. Although this provides employment opportunities and makes money for local communities, the treatment and care of captive elephants is a concern. Some of Thailand's captive elephants are cared for ethically in sanctuaries. But many elephants are mistreated. They are forced to perform or interact with tourists, which can be stressful for the animals.

ETHICAL ELEPHANT TOURISM

The best way to ethically visit elephants in Thailand is in national parks such as Kui Buri and Khao Yai. This is where people can see elephants in the wild. If visitors want to visit captive elephants in Thailand, they should find places that prioritize the animals' well-being. Elephants should not be forced to interact with people or perform tricks. Ethical elephant sanctuaries will usually allow tourists to look at but not touch the animals.

Currently, more than half of Thailand's 7,000 elephants live in captivity.[7] In the wild, increasing loss of habitat threatens elephants. Conflicts can also arise between humans and elephants in places where natural habitats border agricultural areas. Elephants can damage crops such as rice and cassava. People sometimes use guns or electric fences to keep elephants from their fields. This can result in elephant deaths.

The Elephant Nature Park in Chiang Mai is one place where tourists can see Thailand’s elephants.

Some of Thailand's rivers run through heavily forested areas.

FOREST BIOMES

Forests in Thailand can be evergreen or deciduous. The type of forest in a region depends on the location's elevation, temperature, and amount of moisture. In the north, forests include both deciduous and evergreen trees. The southern peninsula contains mostly evergreens.

The two major types of evergreen forests in Thailand are tropical evergreen forests and pine forests. Tropical evergreen forests, including tropical rainforests, are found throughout the country in areas with heavy rainfall. The tallest rainforest trees stretch more than 100 feet (30 m) high.[8] Smaller plants, including bamboos, palms, and rattans, live in the shade of the taller trees. Ferns and mosses grow on tree trunks and branches.

The other type of evergreen forest is pine forest. These forests are found in the northern regions. They are home to two species of tropical pine trees, the two-needle pine and the three-needle pine.

THAILAND'S GIANT CORPSE FLOWER

Thailand is home to the second-largest flower species in the world, *Rafflesia kerrii*. Its blooms can measure up to 43 inches (110 cm) across.[10] This flower grows in the rainforests of southern Thailand, most notably in Khao Sok National Park. Rafflesias are known as corpse flowers for their putrid odor. They bloom once a year for only a few days. During that time, they emit a smell like rotting flesh. This odor attracts flies, which pollinate the flowers.

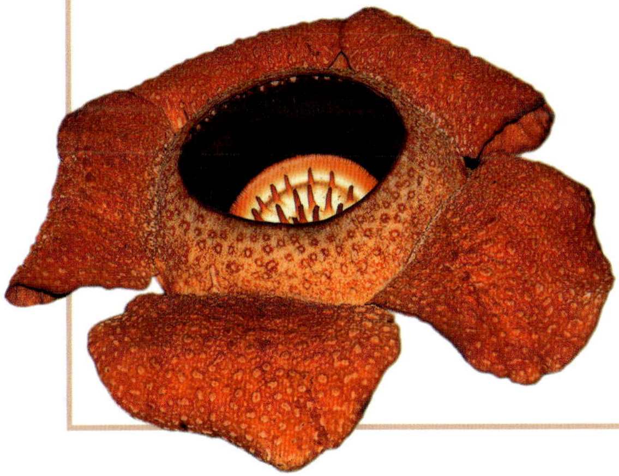

Deciduous forests are found throughout the country. They can be subdivided into two types, mixed deciduous forests and dry dipterocarp forests. Mixed deciduous forests have trees valued for their timber, such as teak and rosewood. Bamboos and grasses grow beneath these larger trees. Dry dipterocarp forests are named for their predominant species, which are trees in the dipterocarp family. These tall hardwood trees are used for their resin and timber. Dry dipterocarp forests are commonly found in more arid regions where annual rainfall is less than 39 inches (100 cm).[9]

Thailand's forests are home to large populations of wildlife. This includes mammals such as elephants, tigers, clouded leopards, Malayan tapirs, wild oxen, gibbons, macaques, and binturongs. Forest birds range from tiny nectar-eating sunbirds to great hornbills that have wingspans of nearly five feet (1.5 m).[11] Reptiles and amphibians found in forests include geckos, chameleons, king cobras, reticulated pythons, and many frog species. Thailand's forests also have many kinds of insects, including various butterflies, beetles, and grasshoppers.

FRESHWATER BIOMES

Thailand also has significant freshwater biodiversity due to its many rivers, streams, ponds, swamps, and floodplains. The country has more than 14,138 square miles (36,616 sq km) of freshwater wetland.[12] Aquatic plants such as lotuses and water lilies are common in these habitats.

Thailand's freshwater biomes support 120 species of birds and more than 180 species of reptiles and amphibians, as well as many mammals. Some of these animals are endangered, including the Irrawaddy dolphin, Siamese crocodile, and smooth-coated otter. In addition, an estimated 10 percent of the world's freshwater fish species are found in Thailand. Scientists have recorded at least 858 freshwater fish species in Thai waters.[13] One of these is the giant catfish. It is known locally as *pla buek*. This species lives in the Mekong River and may be the largest freshwater fish in the world. It can grow up to 9.8 feet (3 m) long and weigh about 660 pounds (300 kg).[14]

Thailand's freshwater biomes face threats such as the construction of dams and water diversion projects. Development and urbanization in the Chao Phraya River basin during recent decades have reduced biodiversity in the area. Some species have disappeared from the basin, such as the shovelnose sea catfish and the Siamese tiger fish.

The development of infrastructure along the Mekong River has threatened the giant catfish, but conservationists are working to protect the species.

MARINE BIOMES

Thailand's coasts along the Andaman Sea and Gulf of Thailand have varied habitats with important environmental roles. These regions also support people's livelihoods through the fishing and tourism industries. Yet human activities threaten the delicate balance of these marine biomes.

Coral reefs are found along both of Thailand's coasts. They are home to many fish, such as clown fish and moray eels, as well as marine invertebrates. These animals depend on coral reefs for

Thailand celebrates National Mangrove Forest Day on May 10, highlighting the importance of these vital coastal ecosystems.

shelter and food. Coral reefs provide people with jobs and recreation. They also protect the coast from storm surges and erosion. Thailand's largest area of coral reefs is in the Surat Thani Province on the Gulf of Thailand.

About one-third of Thailand's coastlines are bordered by mangrove forests.[15] Mangrove forests provide food, shelter, and nursery grounds for many fish and bird species. They also support the coastline and protect it from erosion and tropical storms. Like other forests, mangrove forests help fight climate change by trapping carbon that would otherwise be released into the air.

Seagrass meadows are found offshore in both the Andaman Sea and the Gulf of Thailand. They serve as nursery grounds for juvenile fish and important food sources for dugongs, sea turtles, and aquatic birds. Seagrasses stabilize the seafloor and help protect coral reefs and coastal lands from tropical storms. Pollution and harmful fishing methods threaten these habitats.

Beach forests are another important habitat in coastal areas. These forests usually have creeping plants closer to the beach, with low shrubs and larger trees farther inland. Beach forests protect sandy beaches against erosion and the effects of winds and storms. This is important for several sea turtle species that nest on Thailand's beaches. Thailand's beach forests are small, disconnected, and under stress from human activities.

The open waters off Thailand's coasts are home to abundant marine life. Multiple species of dolphins and whales are found here, such as striped dolphins and sperm whales. Other marine species include blacktip reef sharks, manta rays, leopard sharks, and whale sharks, the largest fish in the world.

CHAPTER **FOUR**

HISTORY

People have lived in what is now Thailand for thousands of years. The earliest evidence of modern humans in Thailand consists of stone tools and rock paintings. Scientists believe these artifacts date to between 40,000 and 27,000 years ago.

Ban Chiang in northeast Thailand is considered the most important prehistoric settlement in Southeast Asia. The archaeological site here was once a village and burial place. It was occupied from about 2100 BCE to 200 CE. The site has some of the earliest evidence of farming and metal manufacturing in Southeast Asia. The people of Ban Chiang cultivated rice, domesticated farm animals, made pottery, and created technology to make bronze tools.

In early historical times, a succession of tribal groups controlled Thailand. The first of these were the Mon.

A museum at Ban Chiang preserves ancient artifacts from Thailand's early history.

They came to the region from India around the 200s CE. During the 500s to 800s, the Mon people established Theravada Buddhism as the dominant religion.

Beginning in the 800s, the Khmer empire included much of Southeast Asia. From its capital in modern-day Cambodia, the empire stretched into most of what is now Thailand. Over time, many aspects of Khmer culture were absorbed into or forced upon the population. Khmer influences on Thai art and architecture are still seen today.

Throughout the first millennium, an ethnic group from southwestern China called the Tai migrated south. *Tai* refers to people who speak the Tai language, while *Thai* refers to people from Thailand. Over many centuries, the Tai people settled in what is now Thailand and other parts of Southeast Asia. The first mention of the Tai in this region is an inscription from the 1100s in Cambodia. It refers to them as *syam* or "dark brown" people who are subjects of the Khmer ruler. This is the origin of the name *Siam*, which Thailand was known as until 1939.

THAI KINGDOMS

Thai people date the founding of their nation to 1238. In that year, Tai chieftains declared their independence from the Khmer and Mon kingdoms. They established the first uniquely Thai kingdom at Sukhothai. The Sukhothai Kingdom lasted for nearly 200 years. This is considered a golden era of Thai history. The third Sukhothai king, Ramkhamhaeng the Great, invented the modern Thai alphabet, expanded the kingdom's borders, encouraged artistic expression, and established diplomatic relations with China.

The Si Satchanalai Historical Park in northern Thailand features skeletal remains dating to the Sukhothai Kingdom.

The Sukhothai Kingdom declined in the 1300s. The Ayutthaya Kingdom, founded around 1350, eventually absorbed the Sukhothai Kingdom in the mid-1400s. The Ayutthaya Kingdom was a great power in Southeast Asia for four centuries. The monarchs of this time were absolute rulers and seen as god-kings. The first king of Ayutthaya, Ramathibodi, created a legal code based on Hinduism and traditional Tai customs. During the 1500s, the kingdom of Ayutthaya started diplomatic and commercial relations with Western countries. Thai culture and international trade flourished.

But Ayutthaya's relations with its closest neighbors were less friendly. In 1767, forces from Burma, now called Myanmar, captured Ayutthaya after a 15-month siege. The city was destroyed, as were most of its archives and artworks.

The Burmese did not keep control for long. A young general from Ayutthaya named Phraya Taksin defeated the Burmese occupiers. He became king and established his capital in Thonburi, near the mouth of the Chao Phraya River. General Taksin was overthrown in 1782. A fellow general,

SIAMESE CATS

The Siamese is a breed of cat native to Thailand. They are mostly pale, with darker fur on their feet, tails, faces, and ears. The Siamese is believed to be a very old breed, though its exact origin is a mystery. The first known depiction of Siamese cats comes from a Thai manuscript called the *Tamra Maew*, or "The Cat Book Poems." The manuscript was created during the Ayutthaya period. In Thailand, Siamese cats are called *wichien-maat*, which means "moon diamond." Siamese cats first arrived in the United States and Europe in the 1870s.

RAMA IV, OR KING MONGKUT

Rama IV, also known as King Mongkut, is remembered for his social reforms and for opening Thailand to Western influence. He appointed several Western advisers and assistants to his court. This included Anna Leonowens, an English tutor for his children. Leonowens's account of her experience inspired the 1944 book *Anna and the King of Siam*, which was later adapted into the 1951 musical *The King and I*. The film version of this musical was released in 1956. It is banned in Thailand because the portrayal of King Mongkut is deemed inaccurate and disrespectful. In the movie, the king is depicted as ignorant and vain, rather than as a reformer.

Chao Phraya Chakri, was named king. Chakri was crowned Rama I and founded the Chakri dynasty. The modern-day Thai royal family are members of this dynasty. Rama I established Bangkok as the capital and built the Grand Palace.

Rama I reigned until 1809. His descendants held power after him. Rama II continued restoration efforts and renewed contacts with foreign nations. Rama III took the throne in 1824, fully reopening relations with Western countries and negotiating trade treaties with the United States and China.

Rama IV became king in 1851, and Rama V's reign began in 1868. They faced rising European expansionism. Both sought to incorporate Western influences and modernize their country through European-style social and economic reforms. Their diplomacy and reforms are often credited with helping Thailand avoid European colonization. During their reigns, Thailand lost some of its lands to Britain and France. But Thailand remained the only Southeast Asian nation not colonized by European powers. The reign of Rama VI began in 1910. It was also marked by social reforms, including the introduction of compulsory education.

THE END OF ABSOLUTE MONARCHY

Rama VII was king from 1925 to 1935. He was the last of Thailand's absolute monarchs. In 1932, military officers and other government officials led a nonviolent coup to take power. A constitutional monarchy was established. It placed the king in a mostly ceremonial role. Rama VII stepped down in 1935 and passed the throne to his nephew, Rama VIII. Rama VIII remained king until 1946.

Since 1932, political power has passed between rival groups of military and bureaucratic elites. Often led by powerful generals, these groups have initiated repeated coups. Thailand's powerful military has imposed prolonged periods of martial law. There have been short periods of civilian rule. But progress toward a stable, democratic system of government has been inconsistent during Thailand's recent history.

Following a coup in 1947, the military stayed in power until 1973. During this time, Thailand allied with the United States against the spread of communism. Starting in the 1980s, Thailand's foreign policy priorities shifted. The country emphasized and promoted regional trade relationships. Thailand forged closer economic

FROM SIAM TO THAILAND

Neighbors of the Kingdoms of Sukhothai and Ayutthaya referred to the region as Siam. In the 1500s, the Portuguese adopted this name, and it became widely used. In 1939, a military dictator named Luang Phibunsongkhram ruled Thailand. As part of his nationalist policies, he changed the country's official name from Siam to Thailand. The change was meant to modernize the nation and highlight its people's unique identity.

Military coups became frequent occurrences in Thailand in the 1900s and early 2000s.

ties with Japan and China. Thailand also renewed trade relationships with other Southeast Asian nations, such as Vietnam, Laos, and Cambodia.

Thailand continued to experience political turmoil in the early 2000s. This included a military coup in 2006 and major street protests from 2008 to 2010. Months of anti-government protests in 2014 were followed by another military coup. The junta that took control wrote a new constitution that cemented the military's political power.

Thailand has had 20 different constitutions since 1932.[1]

The popular King Rama IX, whose reign began in 1946, died in 2016. He was succeeded by his son, Rama X. Political instability increased after the

MINI **BIO**

RAMA IX

Thailand's longest-reigning monarch was Rama IX, also known as King Bhumibol Adulyadej. Bhumibol was born in Cambridge, Massachusetts, in 1927. His father was studying at Harvard University at the time. Bhumibol was educated in Switzerland. He enjoyed photography and painting and was an accomplished saxophone player and composer. He succeeded his older brother to the throne at age 18, taking the name Rama IX. For the first few years of his reign, Thailand was ruled by a regent, or substitute, while Rama IX completed his studies in Switzerland. As a constitutional monarch, Rama IX had limited government powers. His most important role was serving as a living symbol of unity for the nation. However, he also mediated infighting among Thailand's divided political parties. Rama IX maintained the monarchy's influence amid political turmoil, a dozen coups, and periods of military rule. He was viewed as a positive and stabilizing force in Thailand. Rama IX was also very popular among the Thai people. He enjoyed widespread public support during his 70-year reign.

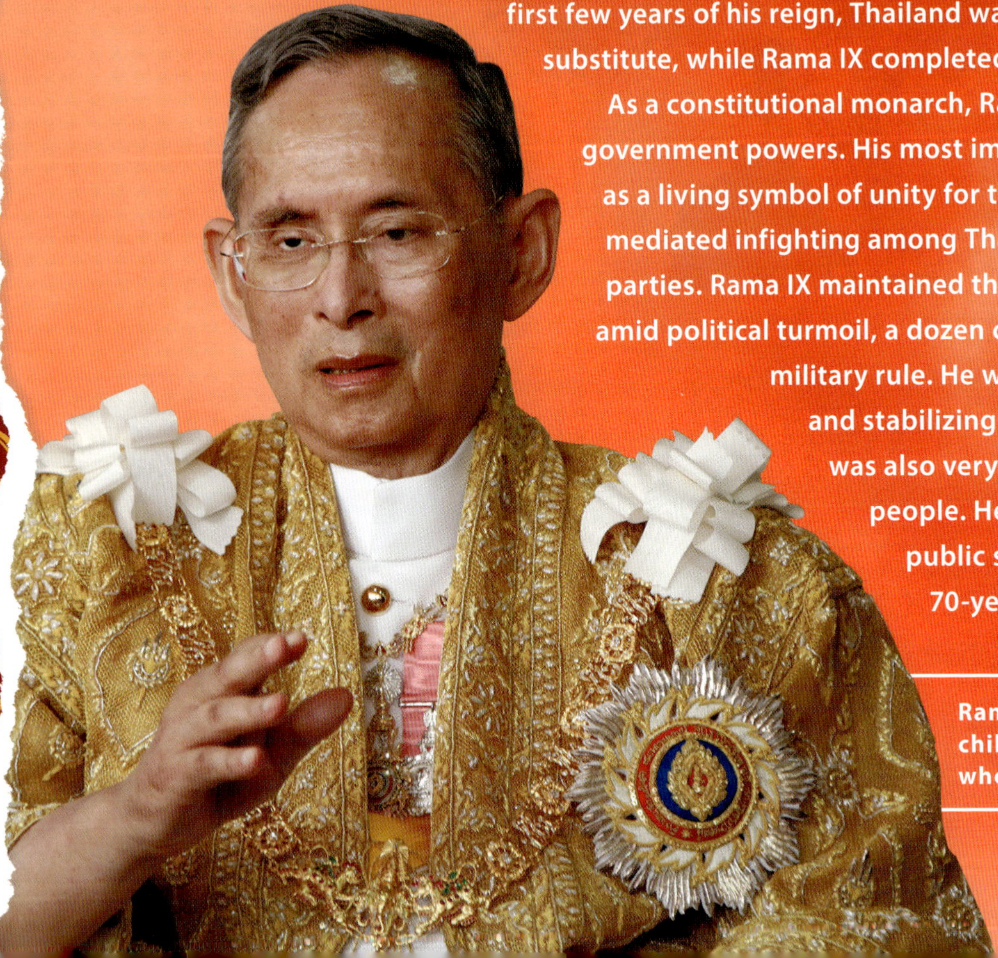

Rama IX had four children, including a son who became Rama X.

death of Rama IX. In 2020, young activists led a wave of anti-government protests across Thailand. They called for democratic reforms and limits on the military's political influence. The government cracked down on these protests and arrested protesters.

RECENT THAI HISTORY

On December 26, 2004, a 9.1-magnitude earthquake struck off the coast of the Indonesian island of Sumatra. The earthquake triggered a tsunami, a series of giant waves that traveled out across the Indian Ocean. The tsunami devastated the coasts of Thailand as well as Indonesia, other countries in South and Southeast Asia, and eastern and southern Africa. It was the deadliest tsunami in recorded history. Approximately 225,000 people were killed across all these regions together.[2]

In Thailand, about 5,400 people lost their lives, including many foreign tourists.[3] The tsunami caused extensive damage to homes, land, and livelihoods. Villages, fishing grounds, and farmlands were destroyed. So were many hotels and resorts. The Thai government led an immediate and effective response to the humanitarian crisis. The Thai public, local businesses, and local charitable organizations contributed to relief efforts in the aftermath of the tsunami. International organizations also helped support rebuilding and recovery.

Thailand was in the international spotlight again in June and July of 2018. A Thai boys' soccer team and their coach had become trapped inside the Tham Luang cave system. Sudden monsoon rains had caused flooding within the long and winding cave, stranding them underground. After nine days, rescue divers located the boys, ages 11 to 16, and their coach deep within the cave.

The successful rescue of the Thai soccer team required an immense concentration of expertise, resources, and effort.

But heavy rains made getting the group out challenging. The world watched as Thai military and government groups worked with a team of international responders to plan a rescue. They pumped water out of the cave to make parts of it more accessible. They also used scuba masks, oxygen canisters, stretchers, and a makeshift system of ropes and slides to guide the boys out of the caves.

Many people came together for the dangerous operation. One volunteer, a former Thai Navy SEAL, died while helping with the rescue. But it was a success. After 18 days trapped in the cave, all 12 boys and their coach made it out alive.[4]

Like the rest of the world, Thailand was significantly affected by the global COVID-19 pandemic. In early 2020, the Thai government instituted a national response. It included early screening of travelers coming into the country and quarantining those who tested positive for the respiratory disease. These steps helped contain the pandemic in 2020. Case and death counts were relatively low for most of that year. The government also implemented economic policies to help people during the early pandemic. These policies included health-related spending and financial assistance for affected households.

Despite these efforts, Thailand's economy was hit hard by the pandemic. This was especially true for the tourism and hospitality industries. The country was completely closed to visitors from March 2020 through June 2021. Tourism returned after the 2021 reopening, but by 2024 it had not yet reached its pre-pandemic level.

CHAPTER FIVE

PEOPLE AND CULTURE

Thailand's approximately 70 million people come from many ethnic groups.[1] The Thai people make up most of the population. Large minority groups include Chinese and Malay people. Other groups include the Khmer and the Mon.

Many distinct Indigenous cultures exist throughout Thailand. Indigenous fishing communities and small populations of hunter-gatherers live in the south. Other small Indigenous communities live on the Khorat Plateau in the northeast. In the north live the seminomadic groups called hill tribes.

Thailand officially recognizes nine of the hill tribes as Indigenous peoples of the nation. They are the Hmong, Karen, Lisu, Mien, Akha, Lahu, Lua, Thin,

About 98 percent of people in Thailand are ethnically Thai.

Thai boys under age 20 can become novice monks.

and Khmu. Most people in these groups live as fishers or hunter-gatherers. They maintain their own languages, customs, and beliefs.

RELIGIONS AND LANGUAGES

Theravada Buddhism is by far the most common religion in Thailand. About 93 percent of the country's population is Theravada Buddhist.[2] Monks are an important and respected part of this school of Buddhism. Nearly every settlement in Thailand has at least one temple where monks live and community rituals take place.

SPIRITS AND SPIRIT HOUSES

Thailand is primarily a Buddhist country. But ideas from animism, Hinduism, and Taoism also figure heavily in Thai culture. One of these ideas is the belief in spirits. Many Thai people believe that spirits, known as *phi*, are everywhere. These spirits inhabit not only the land and parts of the natural world, including rivers and trees, but also household objects.

Most Thai homes, businesses, and public spaces have a spirit house outside. A spirit house looks like a miniature home placed on top of a pole. It is a shrine to the protective spirit or spirits of a place. At spirit houses, people leave offerings such as flowers, incense, and food.

While Buddhism is the dominant religion in Thailand, other major religions are practiced throughout the country. Thailand has a long history of permitting religious freedom. In 1878, the country enacted the Edict of Religious Tolerance. This allowed individuals to choose their religion without restriction from the government. Every constitution of Thailand since has included this freedom. The current constitution prohibits religious discrimination.

The second-largest religion in Thailand is Islam. More than 5 percent of the people of Thailand belong to this faith.[3] Most Muslims who live in Thailand are ethnic Malay and reside in the south near the Malaysian border. Nationwide, Muslim populations also include the descendants of immigrants from South Asia, China, Cambodia, and other places.

Christianity is practiced by about 1 percent of the population. Most of these people are ethnic Chinese, and more than half of the country's Christians are Roman Catholic. Other religions together add up to approximately 1 percent of Thailand's population.[4] These include animism, Confucianism, Hinduism, Judaism, Sikhism, and Taoism.

Thai is the official language of Thailand. It belongs to the Tai language family of Southeast Asia. It is a tonal language. This means that different sounds are used to distinguish between otherwise identical words. Thai has five tones: rising, falling, mid, high, and low. The Thai alphabet has 44 consonants and 32 vowels.[5] Written Thai is read from left to right, with spaces indicating punctuation. Spaces are not put between words. Over the centuries, the language has incorporated foreign words. These include words from Chinese, Sanskrit, Khmer, Portuguese, and English.

More than 94 percent of people in Thailand age 15 and older can read and write.[6]

The Thai language is taught in all the country's schools and used in print and broadcast media. Nearly everyone in Thailand can speak and write Thai. English is a common secondary language in large cities and other tourist destinations.

THAI CUSTOMS

Thai culture is known for being tolerant, friendly, and polite. As in other cultures, people follow certain social norms and etiquette rules. In Thai society, it is important to show respect for the monarchy and religion. It is taboo to say anything critical or improper about the royal family or Buddhism. To most Thai people, the King and his family are living symbols of the nation.

Buddhist monks are also highly respected in Thailand. People typically give their seats to monks on public transportation. It is inappropriate for anyone to touch a monk. Monks are considered sacred, as are images of the Buddha and Buddhist temples. Temple visitors are required to cover their legs and arms when visiting any temple and remove their shoes before entering.

Thai people are known for being open-minded and proud of their freedoms. Yet they are conservative in some regards. It is considered proper etiquette to dress modestly. Even outside of temples, revealing clothing is frowned upon. Thai people are also modest about public displays of affection. Romantic couples tend to avoid hugging or kissing in public places.

Thailand has social norms regarding the head and the feet. Thai people consider the head to be the cleanest and most sacred part of the body. Therefore, Thai people believe one should never touch anyone's head or even tousle a child's hair. It is also disrespectful to touch the head of a statue, especially a statue of the Buddha. As the lowest part of the body, feet are deemed to be dirty. People should always take their shoes off before

THE *WAI* GESTURE

The *wai* is the traditional and common greeting used in Thailand. Generally, it is done by placing the palms of the hands together at chest level and bowing slightly. However, there are complex rules and variations of the gesture that depend on the relationship between the people involved. A person can indicate different levels of respect with the height of their hands or the depth of their bow.

entering a Thai house or temple. In addition, it is considered vulgar to put feet up on a table. Feet should never be pointed at food, people, or images of the Buddha. It is even considered rude to use one's foot to stop a fallen coin from rolling away, since coins bear the king's image.

Another important aspect of the Thai character is the expectation that people will remain calm, even in frustrating situations. In Thailand, outbursts are considered rude and reflect poorly on a person. They also embarrass other people. Instead of getting angry or impatient, the Thai people value staying lighthearted. People tend to keep their cool, avoid confrontation, and use humor to calm tense situations. The Thai expression for this is *jai yen*, which translates to "cool heart."

ENTERTAINMENT AND RECREATION

Traditional Thai events and festivals take place throughout the year. Many have religious aspects. Some other festivals originated from traditional beliefs and folklore.

One of the most important events is Songkran, or the Thai New Year festival. It is celebrated in April. During Songkran, people spend time with their families and honor older adults and ancestors. Water plays a major role in the festival. People celebrate Songkran with giant, friendly water fights in the streets. The Thai throw water from buckets and use squirt guns to playfully splash one another. Symbolically, the splashing washes away misfortunes from the previous year and brings luck in the new year.

Loi Krathong is another major festival in Thailand. It typically takes place on the night of a full moon in November. It was originally a ritual to honor and ask forgiveness from the Water Goddess.

Massive squirt gun fights are a part of some people's Songkran celebrations.

MINI **BIO**

SAMART PAYAKAROON

Muay Thai fighter Samart Payakaroon is considered one of the greatest combat sport athletes of all time. He is known for his quick reflexes and creative, unpredictable fighting style. His nickname is Jade-Faced Tiger. He earned it through his handsome appearance and because he never received any cuts on his face in the ring.

Samart was born in 1962 and started training in Muay Thai at age 11. He began competing in matches at Lumpinee Stadium in Bangkok in 1978. Between 1980 and 1981, Samart won the Lumpinee Stadium Championship in four different weight divisions. In the 1980s, he competed in Muay Thai and professional boxing at the same time, reaching top levels in both sports. Also during this time, Samart launched a music and acting career in Thailand.

Samart competed in 150 Muay Thai matches. He won 130 of these, 30 of them by knockout. His boxing record includes 23 fights and 21 wins, with 12 knockouts.[7] Samart continues to be active in the entertainment industry. He also established his own Muay Thai training camp, the Samart Payakaroon Gym.

The WBC World Championship belt is among the many accolades won by Samart Payakaroon in his fighting career.

People celebrate Loi Krathong by releasing illuminated floating baskets onto bodies of water. This festival is considered a time of joy, gratitude, and new beginnings.

Thai food is all about creating balance between five flavors: sweet, sour, salty, bitter, and spicy. Common seasonings include coconut milk, shrimp paste, garlic, chili peppers, lemongrass, ginger, and lime juice. Rice is a fundamental part of most Thai meals. Dishes also often include barbecued meat and seafood. Thai cuisine has incorporated and adapted influences from other cultures, such as stir-fry dishes and noodles originating from China and curries from India. The regions of Thailand have their own food traditions. For instance, the food in the south tends to be very spicy and include a lot of seafood.

Thailand's national sport is the martial art Muay Thai, also known as Thai boxing. Competitors can target any part of the body with blows from the arms and legs. Muay Thai fighters compete in their bare feet with boxing gloves on their hands. Before a match begins, the boxers perform a dance called the *ram muay*. This honors their teachers and the guardian spirit of Muay Thai. An orchestra of gongs, drums, and wind instruments also plays before and during matches.

EDIBLE INSECTS

Insects have been part of the Thai diet for centuries. Common edible insects include locusts, silkworm pupae, bamboo caterpillars, crickets, and giant water bugs. Insects are often deep-fried or seasoned with spices and sold by street vendors. They are also used as ingredients in stir-fries and other dishes. Edible insects are excellent sources of protein, fat, and vitamins.

The exact origins of Muay Thai are unknown. Many believe the sport evolved from hand-to-hand combat training used by the Thai military in the Sukhothai period. Thai soldiers have trained in Muay Thai for centuries. Official rules and regulations for the sport were created in the 1930s, including the introduction of time limits and boxing gloves. People all over the world now compete in Muay Thai.

Diverse cultures have influenced Thai art throughout history. Traditional Thai art was heavily influenced by Buddhism. Many temples contain sculptures and mural paintings depicting the life of the Buddha or other Buddhist stories. The temples themselves are often decorated with glass mosaics, gilding, porcelain, and mother-of-pearl inlays. Hindu traditions also influenced early Thai art. The *Ramakien* is a Thai version of the Hindu epic *Ramayana*. The Grand Palace in Bangkok has murals portraying this story. Contemporary Thai art incorporates influences from around the globe. Modern paintings, sculptures, and architecture often combine traditional Thai designs and themes with Western styles.

Traditional Thai performing arts are also influenced by Buddhist and Hindu literature. One of these is the *khon*, a classical masked dance. It depicts stories from the *Ramakien*. This art form is culturally and historically significant. It is often performed at royal and religious ceremonies. Thai classical music called *dontri Thai doem* may accompany khon performances. This music was originally played at the royal court and is based on Khmer music. Shadow plays, or *nang talung*, are another traditional Thai dramatic art. These are still performed in the south of Thailand. They use puppets made from water buffalo hides to tell folklore stories.

Thailand's khon performances blend music, dance, handicrafts, and storytelling.

Today, modified versions of Western pop, rock, and rap music are popular in Thailand. King Rama IX, an accomplished saxophonist, popularized jazz music in the nation. Many people also enjoy a type of Thai country music that originated in rural central Thailand. It is called *phlaeng luk thung*, which translates to "songs of the children of the fields."

Thailand is known for several traditional crafts. Silk from Thailand has long been valued for its range of colors and designs. The country is also famous for silverwork. Bangkok is a major center for jewelry made with silver and regionally mined gemstones, such as rubies and sapphires.

CHAPTER **SIX**

POLITICS

Thailand is a constitutional monarchy with a king as the head of state. King Rama X became king in 2016. Thailand's constitution limits the power of the monarch. Kings are mostly a symbol of Thai identity and unity.

The head of government is the prime minister. The prime minister selects people to serve as ministers to lead different sectors of Thailand's government. Together, the prime minister and the other ministers are called the Council of Ministers or the Cabinet. The Cabinet oversees day-to-day government activities and is responsible for setting governmental policy and goals. In Thailand, a person can serve as prime minister for up to eight years.

Thailand's constitution sets out the structure for the country's National Assembly. This is the legislative

Paetongtarn Shinawatra took office as prime minister in August 2024.

The National Assembly complex is located along the Chao Phraya River in Bangkok.

branch of the government, and it is responsible for making laws. The National Assembly has two divisions, which are called the Senate and the House of Representatives. The House of Representatives has members who serve four-year terms. Some are elected directly, while others are elected from party lists based on the proportion of votes that each party receives. Thailand has had universal suffrage since 1932. This means all citizens who are 18 and older can vote in the nation's elections.

The members of the Senate serve five-year terms. Senators were previously selected by the military. But in May 2024, a new selection process came into effect. A total of 200 senators are elected from 20 social and professional groups, with ten members from each group.[1] These groups represent a mix of professions and identities, such as educators, farmers, business owners, and women. Only candidates for the Senate can vote in this election. The candidates vote among themselves in several rounds, with the top vote-getters becoming senators.

The judicial system in Thailand combines elements of traditional Thai and Western laws. There are four types of courts: the Constitutional Court, the Administrative Court, the Military Court, and the Court of Justice. The Court of Justice has general authority over civil and criminal matters. It is divided into three levels, with the highest being the Supreme Court. The Constitutional Court decides on the legality of bills or laws and verifies the qualifications of members of the National Assembly and other government workers. The Administrative Court oversees matters involving state agencies, officials, or contracts. The Military Court hears cases concerning military officers or military laws.

NATIONAL SYMBOLS

Thailand has several national symbols. Many of them are associated with the monarchy and religion. For example, the colors of Thailand's flag—red, white, and blue—have symbolic meanings. Red represents the blood Thai people have shed for their country. White symbolizes the purity of Buddhism. Blue stands for the monarchy.

Previous versions of Thailand's flag featured a white elephant. Elephants, and especially white elephants, have long been associated with good fortune. Elephants were officially recognized as the national animal of Thailand in 2001. However, the animals have been an important national symbol for many centuries. They are associated with the monarchy and Buddhism. Elephants represent traits such as strength, perseverance, and loyalty. Several universities in Thailand feature elephants in their logos. So does the Thai national soccer team, which is known as the War Elephants.

THE THAI NATIONAL ANTHEM

Thailand has had seven national anthems. The first goes back to the reign of King Rama V. The seventh and current anthem is called "Phleng Chat Thai," or "Thai National Anthem." It was adopted in 1939. The music was composed by Phra Chenduriyang and the lyrics are by Luang Saranuprapan. The anthem is played every morning and evening in schools, in offices, and on television and radio. By law, people are required to stand when the national anthem is played.

The Garuda is another national symbol of Thailand. In Hindu mythology, the Garuda is a powerful man-bird hybrid. It serves as the transport of the Hindu god Vishnu. In Thailand, the Garuda is associated with the divine power of the king. It has been an official symbol of the Thai monarchy and government since 1911. The Garuda appears on all Thai legislation and government papers, including the cover of Thai passports. The Garuda is also a symbol of protection in Thai Buddhism.

Thailand's official national mythological creature is the Naga. It is a half-human, half-snake creature from Hindu and Buddhist mythology. Nagas are associated with water and protecting treasure. In Buddhism, Nagas are often depicted as door guardians. They are frequently used to decorate staircase rails leading to Buddhist temples.

CONTEMPORARY THAI POLITICS

Thailand's politics are heavily influenced by three forces: the Buddhist religion, the monarchy, and the military. However, growing frustrations over the roles of the monarchy and the military are present in modern politics. This is especially true among young Thai people. In 2020 and 2021, large pro-democracy demonstrations occurred across Thailand. The government tried to suppress the movement by arresting protesters.

The Thai military has launched 22 coups since 1932. Nineteen of them have been successful.[2]

The demonstrations motivated many Thai voters. Turnout for the May 2023 general election was high. The progressive Move Forward Party received the most votes. This party's platform included a variety of reforms, such as reducing the size of the nation's military and doing away with conscription. Every year, men who are age 21 and older enter a lottery. If chosen, they must serve two years in the military. Support for the practice of conscription, especially among young people, is decreasing. The popularity of the Move Forward Party reflects a shift against the long-standing political power of the military. The party also urged changes in Thailand's laws regarding the royal family.

Though the Move Forward Party won the most votes in the 2023 election, the Senate prevented it from taking power. Following the 2014 coup, the military had appointed conservative senators and written a new constitution. The constitution gave the Senate the power to block a political party from forming a government. The military-appointed senators used this power to deny the Move Forward Party a victory.

Instead, the centrist Pheu Thai Party formed a government. The Pheu Thai Party was the Move Forward Party's biggest coalition partner. But Pheu Thai excluded the Move Forward Party and formed a new partnership with several other political parties. These parties were associated with the previous military-controlled government and were former political rivals of Pheu Thai. Many people viewed this new coalition as a betrayal of the pro-democracy movement. Critics said that Pheu

LÈSE-MAJESTÉ LAW

Thailand's monarchy is protected by a strict lèse-majesté law. This type of law makes it a crime to criticize, insult, or threaten any member of the royal family. In December 2015, a man was even arrested for insulting King Rama IX's dog. Breaking this law can result in up to 15 years in jail. Many Thai people are opposed to the lèse-majesté law. They believe it is used to suppress political expression in Thailand. For instance, during the 2020 political protests, the government charged more than 200 people with violating the law.[3]

Pro-democracy demonstrations have signaled the Thai people's discontent, but the government's power to change the rules and stifle these movements has resulted in little significant change.

Thai replaced Move Forward with military-aligned parties in its coalition government in exchange for an opportunity to win more political power.

The Thai legislature elected a former businessman named Srettha Thavisin as prime minister in August 2023. Around the same time, the Pheu Thai Party's billionaire leader, Thaksin Shinawatra, returned to Thailand after 15 years in exile. Thaksin had been the prime minister in 2006 until he was overthrown by a military coup. Following the coup, Thaksin left the country to avoid charges of insulting the monarchy. Critics believe that a deal might have been made between Thaksin and the military to allow him to return to Thailand.

MARRIAGE EQUALITY

In September 2024, Thailand legalized same-sex marriage. The country's marriage equality bill was supported by the monarchy and a majority of legislators. It granted rights to all married couples regardless of gender. Thailand was the first Southeast Asian nation to recognize same-sex marriage. It was the third nation in Asia to do so, after Taiwan and Nepal.

CONTINUING POLITICAL TURMOIL

To many progressive voters, Pheu Thai appeared to have abandoned its promises to moderate the political influence of the military and the monarchy. This increased the popularity of the Move Forward Party, now Pheu Thai's biggest challenger. But in August 2024, Thailand's Constitutional Court ordered that the Move Forward Party dissolve. The judges ruled that the party had violated the constitution by campaigning to amend a law against criticizing the monarchy. The Move Forward Party quickly regrouped as the People's Party. It remains the main progressive opposition to Pheu Thai and other conservative parties that support the monarchy and military.

Later in August 2024, Thailand's Constitutional Court issued another major ruling. The court ordered the immediate removal of Prime Minister Srettha Thavisin from office over an ethical violation. The judges cited Srettha's appointment of a cabinet member who had been convicted of bribery and jailed for six months. Srettha had served as prime minister for less than a year.

Srettha was replaced by Paetongtarn Shinawatra. Paetongtarn is the third member of her family to serve as prime minister. She is the daughter of Thaksin Shinawatra. Her aunt, Yingluck Shinawatra, was Thailand's first female prime minister, serving from 2011 to 2014. At 37, Paetongtarn became Thailand's youngest prime minister. She was expected to continue the political dynasty founded by her father.

Srettha Thavisin was Thailand's fourth prime minister in 16 years to be removed from office after rulings from the country's Constitutional Court.[4]

CHAPTER **SEVEN**

ECONOMICS

Thailand has the second-largest economy in Southeast Asia, behind Indonesia. In 2023, Thailand's gross domestic product (GDP) was $514.9 billion.[1] The country has a free-market economy, well-developed infrastructure, and a growing middle class. The rates of unemployment and poverty are low.

Only a generation ago, Thailand was a low-income country. But the country has experienced many big economic developments over the last several decades. The Thai government managed to reduce poverty significantly, with the rate dropping from 58 percent in 1990 to 6.8 percent in 2020.[2] Thailand implemented a nationwide minimum wage policy and lowered taxes for middle-income earners in 2013.

Thailand has also made progress in social welfare developments. Compared with a few decades ago,

Bangkok's many skyscrapers, including the distinctive King Power Mahanakhon building, *right*, are visual evidence of the nation's economic success.

Thailand's biggest port is Laem Chabang, located southeast of Bangkok.

In 2023, the unemployment rate in Thailand was just 1 percent.[3]

children are receiving more years of education. Health insurance and other forms of social security have expanded to cover more people. Today, Thailand is considered an upper-middle-income country.

ECONOMIC GROWTH AND TRADE

Until recent decades, the Thai economy was based mostly on agriculture. In the early 1980s, more than two-thirds of Thailand's export earnings came from farming. Less than one-third of its earnings came from manufacturing. The government began encouraging the shift away from agriculture and toward the manufacturing industry in the 1960s. Over time, Thailand increased its production and export of textiles, consumer goods, and electronic parts. By the early 2000s, agriculture accounted for only one-eighth of export earnings, and it made up just one-tenth of the nation's GDP.[4] The other 90 percent of GDP came from the industrial and service sectors.[5]

The Thai economy was one of the fastest growing in the world between 1963 and 1997. During these years, the economy grew at an average annual rate of 7.5 percent. The Asian financial crisis of 1997 briefly slowed this economic growth. In response, the government increased spending on infrastructure and economic stimulus measures. These actions, along with tourism revenue, helped boost the economy. Following the crisis, the Thai economy grew at an average annual rate of 5 percent between 1999 and 2005.[6]

Thailand's current economy is heavily dependent on international trade. Exports account for much of the country's GDP. Thailand's main exports are electronics, agricultural machine parts, vehicles and their parts, and foods. These exports go to countries such as the United States, China, Japan, Vietnam, and Malaysia.

THE ASIAN FINANCIAL CRISIS

The Asian financial crisis began in Thailand in July 1997 when the Thai currency rapidly dropped in value. The crisis soon spread to other Southeast Asian countries, including Indonesia, Malaysia, and the Philippines. These countries saw their currency exchange rates and stock markets plunge. From 1996 to 1997, Thailand's GDP per capita dropped by 21 percent.[7]

By the fall of 1997, the crisis had extended to South Korea, Hong Kong, and China. The Asian financial crisis became a global financial crisis when it spread to the Russian and Brazilian economies in 1998. International stock markets hit record lows. In response, international organizations and governments offered financial support to affected countries in the form of loans. These loans ultimately helped contain the crisis. By 1999, there were signs of recovery in Asian economies.

Given the importance of its exports, Thailand is a leader in Southeast Asia on trade issues. Thailand is a key player and founding member of the Association of Southeast Asian Nations (ASEAN). ASEAN is a political and economic coalition of ten nations in Southeast Asia. It was founded in 1967 to promote economic growth, cultural exchange, stability, and security in the region. Thailand has friendly relationships and growing networks of trade agreements with many other countries in Asia and elsewhere. Its location in the heart of Southeast Asia has made it a regional center for international travel and trade.

NATURAL RESOURCES AND AGRICULTURE

Thailand has an abundant supply of natural resources. Historically, the country was a major exporter of hardwoods. These trees include teak and dipterocarp species. But following the

THE THAI BAHT

Thailand's currency is the baht. The Bank of Thailand issues banknotes in amounts that range from 10 to 1,000 baht. A picture of the reigning king of Thailand is on one side of every banknote, along with other royal symbols. On the other side, different banknotes have varying historical images. For example, the 50-baht note shows a statue of King Rama V.

Each baht is subdivided into 100 satang. Coin amounts range from 25 satang to 10 baht. All newly minted coins depict the current monarch, King Rama X, on the heads side. Coins feature an array of the most famous temples in Thailand on the reverse side.

government's 1989 logging ban, the nation's forested areas have been largely protected. Efforts are being made to conserve the remaining forests in Thailand.

Fish and other marine life are also historically important resources. Thailand has been one of the world's major exporters of fish, shrimp, and fish products since the 1970s. But the creation of shrimp farms and increased fishing in the Gulf of Thailand have caused problems. Many traditional marine fishing areas are polluted and overfished. Shrimp farms have damaged important habitats in southern Thailand, such as mangrove forests.

Thailand is one of the world's largest producers of tin. Tin is mined mostly in the southern peninsula. Other important Thai mineral resources include zinc, tungsten, fluorite, gypsum, limestone, marble, and a type of coal called lignite. Rubies and sapphires are also mined in Thailand.

Thailand's fertile soils and favorable growing conditions have supported agriculture for thousands of years. Today, the agricultural sector of the Thai economy consists mostly of small-scale farms. Agriculture accounts for 10 percent of the country's GDP. But it employs about one-third of the labor force.[8]

Rice is the main staple crop of Thailand. It is also a major agricultural export. Thailand is one of the world's largest exporters of rice. Most rice is grown in the Chao Phraya River basin and the Khorat Plateau. Thailand also produces many other commercial crops. These include cassava, maize, mangoes, pineapples, durians, cashews, vegetables, and flowers. The nation also produces rubber, coffee, and sugarcane.

INDUSTRIES AND SERVICES

Thailand has a strong industrial sector. It accounts for about 40 percent of the nation's GDP.[9] The nation's manufacturing industry began to grow in the 1970s. By the 1980s, most of Thailand's manufacturing involved labor-intensive products meant for export.

This trend continued into the following decades. Since the 1990s, Thailand has been a major exporter of high-technology goods, such as computer components, vehicle parts, and telecommunications equipment. Other manufactured products include jewelry, rubber products, and plastics. Thailand also exports agro-industrial products such as canned and processed foods.

Thailand's service sector includes industries such as tourism, retail, health, finance, communications, and transportation. Architects, engineers, lawyers, and doctors are among the kinds of workers in the service sector. The service industry also includes people working in hotels, shops, and restaurants. Other countries, including some neighboring nations in Southeast Asia, have seen their service sectors grow in recent decades. Thailand's service sector has remained stable during the last two decades. It accounts for about 50 percent of the GDP.[10]

In hilly areas, rice is sometimes grown on terraced fields.

Thailand is working to bring tourists back to its stunning beaches and many other attractions.

ECONOMIC CHALLENGES AND OUTLOOK

Tourism accounts for about 7 percent of Thailand's GDP.[14]

Thailand has made economic and social progress during the last four decades. However, some issues remain. Poverty has been significantly reduced. But it is still a problem, especially in rural areas and in agricultural households. Poverty also varies with geographic region. The poverty rate in southern and northeastern Thailand is almost twice that of the nation as a whole. Economic inequality is also a concern. More than half of the country's wealth is in the hands of the richest 10 percent of the population.[11]

The COVID-19 pandemic slowed economic growth around the world, including in Thailand. By 2023, other Southeast Asian countries showed signs of economic recovery. The GDP of the Philippines, Indonesia, and Vietnam grew by 5 percent or more in 2023. But Thailand's economy grew by just 1.9 percent in that year.[12]

Several factors may contribute to Thailand's slower growth. One is that Thailand's economy is heavily dependent on exports and tourism. This is a problem because the demand for Thai goods and services is relatively weak. Thailand's exports to China, a top trading partner, have slowed. In addition, the tourism industry has not fully recovered from the disruptions associated with the COVID-19 pandemic. In 2023, the number of tourists in Thailand was only about 70 percent of what it had been in 2019.[13] This figure is expected to continue to improve with time, but the sluggish recovery is hurting the economy.

Prime Minister Srettha Thavisin was among the Thai leaders seeking to tackle the nation's economic problems between 2023 and his removal from office in August 2024.

Thailand is also facing an education and skills crisis. The country performs well in terms of how many years of schooling its people receive. But the quality of education remains an issue. Critics say that the education system has failed young Thai people by not adequately preparing them for today's careers. About two-thirds of Thai youth and adults struggle with basic literacy. Three-quarters of Thai people have poor digital literacy skills.[15] And Thailand's English language

ECONOMIC STIMULUS

In September 2024, the ruling Pheu Thai Party initiated a stimulus program worth approximately 450 billion baht ($14 billion) to boost the economy. It involves distributing cash to millions of Thai citizens. Pheu Thai had promised to give handouts of 10,000 baht (about $300) to 45 million people. The government rolled out the program in phases. It started by distributing funds to about 14.5 million people, focusing on some of the most vulnerable populations.[16]

proficiency is relatively low compared with other Southeast Asian countries. The combination of low productivity and poor education means that much of the workforce is limited to low-paid jobs.

Finally, political uncertainty in Thailand poses risks to the economy. The rapid turnover of prime ministers in recent decades may have hurt investor confidence. The prime minister who took office in 2024, Paetongtarn Shinawatra, had no experience serving in government. Her administration faced challenges such as the sluggish economy and decreasing popularity of the Pheu Thai Party. In addition, many people questioned the stability of her government coalition. Pheu Thai came together with its coalition partners to prevent the Move Forward Party from taking power. This foundation may make it difficult for the government to effectively address the nation's issues.

CHAPTER **EIGHT**

THAILAND TODAY

Thailand has undergone significant political and economic developments since the late 1900s. These have been accompanied by social and cultural changes. Traditional influences, such as Buddhism and the monarchy, are still a part of everyday Thai life. But the country has also embraced global ideas and blended them into its culture.

In recent decades, Thailand has experienced increasing urbanization. Many people from rural villages are moving to more urban areas. Additionally, people in rural areas are living more similarly to their urban counterparts than in the past. Government programs brought electricity to most Thai villages in the 1970s and 1980s. Most households now have

In Thailand it is common for large families to live together under one roof.

televisions and other electronics. Modern amenities such as convenience stores and ATMs can be found in villages throughout Thailand. Rural communities are finding it easier to adopt urban lifestyles. Factors such as globalization, digitization, and increased mobility are contributing to this change.

EDUCATION REFORMS

Over the past three decades, Thailand has greatly reformed its educational system. These reforms have expanded access to education, especially in rural and disadvantaged areas. Another aim of the reforms is to improve the quality of schools across the country.

The modern Thai educational system has two key features. First, the government provides all Thai children with 12 years of free education, plus three years of preschool.[2] The second feature is a national curriculum that is shared by all public schools. This curriculum sets educational standards for different grades.

RED BULL

The carbonated, caffeinated energy drink Red Bull was created by a Thai man named Chaleo Yoovidhya. He was born into a poor farming family but moved to Bangkok and started his own company, TC Pharmaceuticals. He developed a drink to keep factory workers and truck drivers alert through long shifts. Chaleo called it *Krating Daeng*, which is Thai for "Red Bull." Austrian businessman Dietrich Mateschitz helped bring the drink to the rest of the world in the 1980s. Red Bull went on to become the world's biggest-selling energy drink and make Chaleo one of the world's richest men. Chaleo died in 2012. His family owns 51 percent of Red Bull, making them worth an estimated $36 billion.[1]

The Thai school curriculum includes academic subjects, moral and ethical education, physical education, and extracurricular activities.

The educational system is divided into three levels. Early childhood education is for children ages three to five. This level includes preschools and kindergartens. The next level is basic education. It includes primary education, which covers grades one through six, and lower secondary education, grades seven through nine. At this level, children study core subjects such as the Thai language, math, science, social studies, and foreign languages. Students continue to the third level, which is upper secondary education, grades ten through twelve. Students may take classes to prepare them for higher education. Or they may follow a vocational education track focusing on technical skills and job training.

Enrollment in Thailand's secondary schools increased from 31 percent of eligible children in 1990 to 78 percent in 2011.[3]

Options for higher education in Thailand include universities, colleges, and vocational institutions. Thailand's first university, Chulalongkorn University, was founded in 1917. Since then, many state and private colleges and universities have been established.

Due to recent reforms, more Thai children have access to basic education. However, the quality of education is an issue. Thailand lags in giving students the skills and knowledge necessary for high-quality jobs. The quality of education is especially problematic in small schools and in rural village schools.

Thailand is trying to solve these problems with reforms to improve the quality and relevance of its educational system. The national curriculum is being updated to emphasize skills such as critical thinking, creativity, and digital literacy. People want to see better teacher training programs and more support for educators throughout their careers. The government is actively promoting science, technology, engineering, and mathematics (STEM) education for Thai students. It is also encouraging more students to develop job skills by enrolling in technical and vocational training programs.

DAILY LIFE FOR YOUNG THAI PEOPLE

Family connections are important in Thailand. Several generations often live together. This arrangement allows extended family members to help raise children. People are expected to respect and obey their elders. Thai people have a strong sense of duty and responsibility toward the elderly.

A typical day for a young Thai person might start with a family breakfast before school. Thai breakfasts commonly include rice, fish and other meats, fruit, and bread. Then the student puts on a school uniform. Uniforms are mandated for students in both public and private schools.

Most children walk to school. Others ride their bikes, take public transportation, or ride school buses. The school year is divided into two semesters. Classes begin in May and end in March. School holidays include all public holidays, Buddhist religious holidays, and some international holidays, such as New Year's Day.

After school, Thai kids participate in clubs and activities, such as bands, dance troupes, and sports teams. They also enjoy playing games. A traditional game called *takraw* is a favorite pastime. Players try to keep a woven rattan ball in the air without using their hands. Takraw is an

THE CONCEPT OF *SANUK*

The Thai word *sanuk* is roughly translated as "fun." But that fails to capture the deep importance of sanuk in Thai culture. Sanuk is a way of life in Thailand. Thai people consider having fun to be a valuable activity. Sanuk can take the form of gentle teasing, wordplay, or just being silly. A common Thai belief is that anything worth doing should have an element of sanuk.

The game of *takraw* requires intense athletic fitness and keen coordination.

internationally competitive sport in Southeast Asia. Formal games are played with a net between two teams of players.

In recent years, video games have experienced a surge of popularity in Thailand. The market for video games is expected to grow as more Thai people gain an interest in gaming. Board games are another popular entertainment option.

CHALLENGES: POLITICS AND HUMAN RIGHTS

Thailand's political instability is a continuing challenge. Elites associated with the monarchy and the military have long held political power in Thailand. Young people, including university students, are putting pressure on the Thai government to be more democratic. Since 2020, large pro-democracy demonstrations have occurred throughout Thailand. Protester demands include changing the constitution and ending injustices in the legal system. Protesters also want limits on the influence of the military and the monarchy in Thai politics.

The calls for democratic reforms challenge the traditional social hierarchy in Thailand. Protesters face strong opposition from older generations, who tend to support the monarchy and defend the importance of the king's role in politics and everyday life. The previous monarch, King Rama IX, was a popular and uniting force in Thailand for 70 years.

Rama X, elevated to the throne after the death of Rama IX in 2016, has been a more controversial figure. Critics say his extravagant lifestyle and spending habits are inappropriate. Rama X has not commanded the respect and reverence of the Thai people to the degree his father did. More Thai people are questioning whether the monarchy is serving their interests or just the interests of the ruling elites.

Thailand, as Siam, voted at the United Nations for the 1948 Universal Declaration of Human Rights. This is an international document listing the rights and freedoms that should be protected for all people. These fundamental rights include the right to be free from slavery and torture, the right to education, and the rights to life, liberty, and privacy. Over the last few decades, however, global human rights organizations have criticized the Thai government and law enforcement agencies for human rights abuses.

Although the country performs well in financial and religious freedom, Thailand has problems with political fairness, freedom of speech, the right to assemble and protest, and equality for vulnerable groups. While Thailand holds elections, they are not entirely free or fair. Critics accuse the king and the military of interfering with political processes. Harassment of political organizations and their members is an issue.

Thailand's constitution guarantees freedom of speech. But the government has restricted this freedom. For example, the government has used the emergency public safety measures

Protests in Thailand have sometimes been met with violent crackdowns.

introduced during the COVID-19 pandemic to limit free speech, with the authorities arresting or intimidating critics. The government also exerts control over content in mainstream media and on the internet.

The Thai government continues to use emergency powers to harass and arrest protesters. There is evidence of authorities attacking, beating, and using live ammunition against demonstrators. Thailand's government has also passed laws restricting the activities of human rights organizations and other groups it considers a national security threat.

Thailand's justice system has problems with government interference, lack of due process, and illegal use of force by law enforcement authorities. Some pro-democracy activists have been detained without a trial for extended periods. International human rights groups have documented the illegal use of torture by Thai security forces, leading to the deaths of prisoners.

The Thai constitution prohibits discrimination based on many factors, including race. However, no laws explicitly address racism and racial discrimination. Thailand has several politically

MIGRANTS AND REFUGEES

Thailand has not signed the 1951 United Nations Convention on Refugees. This means that people seeking asylum in Thailand have fewer rights than in other countries. Thailand does not have an official asylum policy. Refugees have the same legal status as undocumented immigrants.

More than 90,000 refugees from Myanmar live in shelters on the Thai side of the southern border with Myanmar. Thailand is also home to thousands of other refugees from approximately 40 nations.[4] Human rights organizations have criticized the Thai government for mistreatment of people seeking asylum.

marginalized communities, such as Malay Muslims in the south and the Indigenous Karen tribes in the north. These communities experience discrimination and sometimes military violence.

CHALLENGES: THE ENVIRONMENT

Air pollution is a significant threat to public health in Thailand. Chiang Mai, in the north of the country, was ranked as the world's most polluted city in 2023. Throughout northern Thailand, the dry season has become known as the haze season due to the dangerous levels of smog. Some of this smog comes from forest fires. But the biggest source of air pollution is the seasonal burning of rice and sugarcane fields. Farmers use controlled fires to remove undergrowth and fertilize their fields. But in the dry season, there is little wind or rain to remove the resulting haze.

The rate of pollution-related diseases was high in 2023. The toxic smog causes respiratory illnesses and other health issues. People with medical conditions, such as asthma, bronchitis, and heart diseases, are especially vulnerable.

Critics say the Thai government is not doing enough to eliminate the causes of air pollution. Instead, it has focused on treating the symptoms. The country has tried cloud seeding to induce rain to wash out the pollution. This technique involves adding substances to clouds to encourage the formation of precipitation. Officials sometimes urge employees to work from home when pollution levels are high.

In 2023, more than ten million Thai people sought treatment for pollution-related illnesses.[5]

In 2024, the city of Bangkok announced it was partnering with the international Breathe Cities initiative in an effort to significantly improve air quality.

Climate change is another big environmental issue facing Thailand. Certain characteristics make the country more vulnerable to the impacts of climate change. These include its long coastlines, fragile agricultural system, and susceptibility to extreme weather events. Other environmental issues add to Thailand's vulnerability. Air and water pollution, deforestation, and degradation of natural resources may intensify the effects of climate change.

Thailand is already experiencing rising temperatures, harsher droughts, and more frequent and severe floods. These climate hazards are felt nationwide and affect many aspects of Thai society. Climate change affects public health by increasing the risks of respiratory illnesses, malnutrition, and other diseases. Coastal erosion has cost the country an estimated six billion Thai baht ($180 million in 2024) in lost land.[6] Droughts can lead to food and water scarcity, as well as loss of biodiversity. Climate change can also negatively affect important industries such as tourism and agriculture.

Thailand is a land of stunning natural beauty and a rich culture with a long history. Young people in Thailand are using their voices more and more to write the next chapter in the country's story. They are calling for democratic reforms, environmental regulations, and other solutions to the challenges Thailand faces today. Their actions will help determine the nation's future.

ESSENTIAL **FACTS**

OFFICIAL NAME: KINGDOM OF THAILAND

GEOGRAPHY

Area: 198,117 square miles (513,120 sq km)

Highest Elevation: Doi Inthanon at 8,415 feet (2,565 m)

Lowest Elevation: Gulf of Thailand at 0 feet (0 m)

PEOPLE

Population: 69.9 million (2024 est.)

Most Populous City: Bangkok (11 million)

Ethnic Groups: Thai, Burmese, Chinese, Malay, Khmer, Mon, Indigenous groups, other

Religions: Buddhism, Islam, Christianity, other

GOVERNMENT

Type of Government: Constitutional monarchy

Capital: Bangkok

Head of State: King

Head of Government: Prime minister

Legislature: Bicameral, with a Senate and a House of Representatives

ECONOMY

Currency: Baht

Major Industries: Agriculture, fishing, manufacturing, tourism

Natural Resources: Tin, tungsten, coal, zinc, gypsum, fluorite, limestone, marble

NATIONAL SYMBOLS

National Anthem: "Phleng Chat Thai" ("National Anthem of Thailand")

National Animal: Asian elephant

National Mythological Creature: Naga

GLOSSARY

biome

A community of plants and animals that adapt to and live in a specific climate.

coup

An attempt to overthrow government leaders.

deciduous

A type of tree that sheds its leaves annually.

dignitary

A person holding a high rank or office.

free-market economy

An economic system based on supply and demand with little direct government involvement.

gross domestic product (GDP)

The monetary value of all final goods and services produced within a nation's geographic borders over a specified period of time.

isthmus

A narrow strip of land with water on both sides that connects two larger land areas.

junta
A group that controls a government after a revolution.

martial law
The replacement of civilian rule with military control.

monsoon
A seasonal wind in South and Southeast Asia between May and September that brings heavy rain.

pagoda
A tower with many stories, each with its own roof, often built as part of a Buddhist temple.

plateau
An area of level ground that is higher than the surrounding area.

suffrage
The right to vote in a political election.

tuk-tuk
A three-wheeled motor vehicle often used as a taxi.

ADDITIONAL **RESOURCES**

SELECTED BIBLIOGRAPHY

Hafner, James A., et al. "Thailand." *Britannica*, 25 Oct. 2024, britannica.com. Accessed 29 Oct. 2024.

"Thailand Country Profile." *BBC News*, 16 Aug. 2024, bbc.com. Accessed 29 Oct. 2024.

"Thailand in Brief." *Royal Thai Consulate-General, Los Angeles*, 30 Nov. 2022, thaiconsulatela.thaiembassy.org. Accessed 29 Oct. 2024.

FURTHER READINGS

Eimer, David, et al. *Thailand*. Lonely Planet, 2024.

Fodor's Essential Thailand. Fodor's Travel, 2022.

Sonneborn, Liz. *Vietnam*. Abdo, 2026.

ONLINE RESOURCES

Booklinks
NONFICTION NETWORK
FREE! ONLINE NONFICTION RESOURCES

To learn more about Thailand, please visit **abdobooklinks.com** or scan this QR code. These links are routinely monitored and updated to provide the most current information available.

MORE INFORMATION

For more information on this subject, contact or visit the following organizations:

Bangkok National Museum

4 Na Phra That Rd.
Phra Borom Maha Ratchawang, Phra Nakhon
Bangkok 10200 Thailand
finearts.go.th/museumbangkok/

The Bangkok National Museum is home to the largest collection of Thai art and artifacts in the country. Located on the grounds of the Grand Palace in Bangkok, it was established in 1887 by King Rama V.

Tourism Authority of Thailand

1600 Phetchaburi Rd.
Makkasan, Ratchathevi
Bangkok 10400 Thailand
tourismthailand.org/home

The Tourism Authority of Thailand was established in 1979 under the Ministry of Tourism and Sports to promote the country's tourism industry.

Wildlife Conservation Society, Thailand Program

thailand.wcs.org

The Wildlife Conservation Society (WCS) Thailand Program began in 1980 with the goal of working with the Thai government and local and international organizations to conserve wild places and wildlife in Thailand.

SOURCE **NOTES**

CHAPTER 1. A TOUR OF THAILAND

1. "Bangkok, Thailand Population 2024." *World Population Review*, 2025, worldpopulationreview.com. Accessed 8 Jan. 2025.
2. James Harrison. "Grand Palace." *Britannica*, 26 Jan. 2024, britannica.com. Accessed 8 Jan. 2025.
3. "The Emerald Buddha." *The Grand Palace*, n.d., royalgrandpalace.th. Accessed 8 Jan. 2025.
4. "Wat Pho (Temple of the Reclining Buddha)." *US News & World Report*, n.d., travel.usnews.com. Accessed 8 Jan. 2025.
5. Andreas Walderich. "Number of Buddhist Temples in Thailand from 2021 to 2023." *Statista*, 1 Oct. 2024, statista.com. Accessed 8 Jan. 2025.
6. "Wat Pho (Temple of the Reclining Buddha)." *Thailand Magazine*, n.d., thailandmagazine.com. Accessed 8 Jan. 2025.
7. "Tourist Arrivals Top 28m in 2023." *Bangkok Post*, 2 Jan. 2024, bangkokpost.com. Accessed 8 Jan. 2025.

CHAPTER 2. GEOGRAPHY

1. "Thailand." *CIA World Factbook*, 17 Dec. 2024, cia.gov. Accessed 8 Jan. 2025.
2. "Thailand," *CIA World Factbook*.
3. Jeffrey W. Jacobs et al. "Mekong River." *Britannica*, 3 May 2024, britannica.com. Accessed 8 Jan. 2025.
4. "Chao Phraya River." *Britannica*, 14 Sept. 2023, britannica.com. Accessed 8 Jan. 2025.
5. "Forests and Forestry." *Open Development Thailand*, 15 Dec. 2019, thailand.opendevelopmentmekong.net. Accessed 8 Jan. 2025.
6. "Urbanization." *CIA World Factbook*, n.d., cia.gov. Accessed 8 Jan. 2025.
7. Siriwat Pokrajen. "Thailand." *International Urban and Regional Cooperation*, 3 May 2021, iurc.eu. Accessed 8 Jan. 2025.
8. "Urbanization in Thailand Is Dominated by the Bangkok Urban Area." *World Bank Group*, 26 Jan. 2015, worldbank.org. Accessed 13 Jan. 2025.
9. Yongyut Trisurat, Hiroaki Shirakawa, and John M. Johnston. "Land-Use/Land-Cover Change from Socio-economic Drivers and Their Impact on Biodiversity in Nan Province, Thailand." *PubMed Central*, 21 Dec. 2020, pmc.ncbi.nlm.nih.gov. Accessed 8 Jan. 2025.
10. Charles F. Keyes et al. "Thailand." *Britannica*, 8 Jan. 2025, britannica.com. Accessed 8 Jan. 2025.
11. "Thailand," *CIA World Factbook*.
12. "Khorat Plateau." *Britannica*, 26 Nov. 2024, britannica.com. Accessed 8 Jan. 2025.
13. "Thailand." *WorldData.info*, Jan. 2025, worlddata.info. Accessed 8 Jan. 2025.
14. "Thailand Destinations by Region." *Amazing Thailand*, 2024, tourismthailand.my. Accessed 8 Jan. 2025.
15. "Ang Thong." *Ang Thong National Marine Park*, 2024, angthong.net. Accessed 8 Jan. 2025.
16. "Ecology of Angthong Marine Park." *Angthong National Marine Park*, 2025, angthongmarinepark.com. Accessed 8 Jan. 2025.
17. "General Information on Thailand." *United Nations Economic and Social Commission for Asia and the Pacific*, n.d., unescap.org. Accessed 8 Jan. 2025.
18. Susanne Nam. "Geography and Climate of Thailand." *Moon Travel Guides*, 2025, moon.com. Accessed 8 Jan. 2025.
19. Nam, "Geography and Climate of Thailand."
20. "Thailand Climatology." *Climate Change Knowledge Portal*, 2021, climateknowledgeportal.worldbank.org. Accessed 8 Jan. 2025.

CHAPTER 3. PLANTS AND ANIMALS

1. Nirunrut Pomoim et al. "Vulnerability to Climate Change of Species in Protected Areas in Thailand." *Scientific Reports*, 5 Apr. 2022, nature.com. Accessed 8 Jan. 2025.

2. "Thailand." *Biodiversity Finance Initiative*, 2021, biofin.org. Accessed 8 Jan. 2025.

3. Jarupong Krisanaraj. "Thailand's Tourism Recovery Puts 4 Marine Species Back on Extinction Watchlist." *Nation*, 8 Apr. 2023, nationthailand.com. Accessed 8 Jan. 2025.

4. "Thailand – Country Profile." *Convention on Biological Diversity*, n.d., cbd.int. Accessed 8 Jan. 2025.

5. "Wild Tiger Numbers Increase in Thailand." *World Wildlife Fund*, 29 July 2024, worldwildlife.org. Accessed 8 Jan. 2025.

6. Rebecca Cairns. "Tigers Are Disappearing from Southeast Asia. A Forest in Thailand Is Offering New Hope." *CNN*, 26 July 2024, cnn.com. Accessed 8 Jan. 2025.

7. Donald Frazier. "In Thailand, You Can Ride an Elephant. But Should You?" *New York Times*, 19 June 2019, nytimes.com. Accessed 8 Jan. 2025.

8. "Forests in the Khao Yai National Park." *Khao Yai National Park*, 2021, khaoyainationalpark.com. Accessed 8 Jan. 2025.

9. "Forest Resources of Thailand." *Food and Agriculture Organization of the United Nations*, n.d., fao.org. Accessed 8 Jan. 2025.

10. Channing Sargent. "Rafflesia: Known as the 'Corpse Flower' Due to Its Offending Smell." *One Earth*, 30 May 2024, oneearth.org. Accessed 8 Jan. 2025.

11. "Birds." *Khao Sok National Park*, n.d., khaosok.com. Accessed 8 Jan. 2025.

12. Pratch Rujivanarom. "Thailand's Rich Freshwater Biodiversity Under Threat." *Earth Journalism Network*, 8 Sept. 2022, earthjournalism.net. Accessed 8 Jan. 2025.

13. Rujivanarom, "Thailand's Rich Freshwater Biodiversity Under Threat."

14. "Unique Facts about Thailand." *Country Reports*, n.d., countryreports.org. Accessed 8 Jan. 2025.

15. "Environment and Natural Resources." *Open Development Thailand*, 19 Dec. 2017, thailand.opendevelopmentmekong.net. Accessed 8 Jan. 2025.

CHAPTER 4. HISTORY

1. "Thai King Endorses New Constitution, 20th since 1932." *Al Jazeera*, 6 Apr. 2017, aljazeera.com. Accessed 8 Jan. 2025.

2. Virginia Gorlinski et al. "Indian Ocean Tsunami of 2004." *Britannica*, 26 Dec. 2024, britannica.com. Accessed 8 Jan. 2025.

3. "15 Years On, a Look Back at the Boxing Day Tsunami." *Reuters*, 18 Dec. 2019, reuters.com. Accessed 8 Jan. 2025.

4. Seán Clarke et al. "Thailand Cave Rescue: How Did the Boys Get Out?" *Guardian*, 9 July 2018, theguardian.com. Accessed 8 Jan. 2025.

SOURCE **NOTES** CONTINUED

CHAPTER 5. PEOPLE AND CULTURE

1. "Thailand." *CIA World Factbook*, 17 Dec. 2024, cia.gov. Accessed 8 Jan. 2025.
2. "Thailand."
3. "Thailand."
4. "Thailand."
5. Theppitak Karoonboonyanan. "Standardization and Implementations of Thai Language." *National Electronics and Computer Technology Center*, n.d., nectec.or.th. Accessed 8 Jan. 2025.
6. "Thailand."
7. "Samart Payakaroon: A True Legend of Muay Thai." *Nation*, 24 Oct. 2023, nationthailand.com. Accessed 8 Jan. 2025.

CHAPTER 6. POLITICS

1. "2024 Thai Senate Selection, Explained." *iLaw*, 3 Mar. 2024, ilaw.or.th. Accessed 8 Jan. 2025.
2. "Thai People and the Military." *Jakarta Post*, 17 May 2023, thejakartapost.com. Accessed 8 Jan. 2025.
3. "Thai People and the Military."
4. Alastair McCready. "'Big Shock': Thailand Faces Political Upheaval as PM Removed from Office." *Al Jazeera*, 15 Aug. 2024, aljazeera.com. Accessed 8 Jan. 2025.

CHAPTER 7. ECONOMICS

1. "Thailand." *CIA World Factbook*, 17 Dec. 2024, cia.gov. Accessed 8 Jan. 2025.
2. "The World Bank in Thailand." *World Bank Group*, n.d., worldbank.org. Accessed 8 Jan. 2025.
3. "Thailand Unemployment." *Focus Economics*, n.d., focus-economics.com. Accessed 8 Jan. 2025.
4. James A. Hafner et al. "Thailand." *Britannica*, 8 Jan. 2025, britannica.com. Accessed 8 Jan. 2025.
5. "About Thailand." *Asia-Pacific Economic Cooperation 2022*, n.d., apec2022.go.th. Accessed 8 Jan. 2025.
6. "The World Bank in Thailand."
7. "Asian Financial Crisis." *Corporate Finance Institute*, n.d., corporatefinanceinstitute.com. Accessed 8 Jan. 2025.
8. "Thailand Economy." *Country Reports*, n.d., countryreports.org. Accessed 8 Jan. 2025.
9. "About Thailand."
10. "About Thailand."
11. "The World Bank in Thailand."
12. Vijitra Duangdee. "Thailand's Economy Stumbles as Philippines, Vietnam, Indonesia Race Ahead." *Al Jazeera*, 1 Apr. 2024, aljazeera.com. Accessed 8 Jan. 2025.
13. Andreas Walderich. "Number of International Tourist Arrivals in Thailand from 2015 to 2023." *Statista*, 10 July 2024, statista.com. Accessed 8 Jan. 2025.
14. Andreas Walderich. "Share of Tourism Contribution to the Gross Domestic Product (GDP) Value in Thailand from 2017 to 2022." *Statista*, 8 Oct. 2024, statista.com. Accessed 8 Jan. 2025.
15. Duangdee, "Thailand's Economy Stumbles."
16. "Thailand Kicks Off Bumper Cash Handouts to Boost Ailing Economy." *Financial Times*, 28 Sept. 2024, ft.com. Accessed 8 Jan. 2025.

CHAPTER 8. THAILAND TODAY

1. "Chalerm Yoovidhya & Family." *Forbes*, 2 July 2024, forbes.com. Accessed 8 Jan. 2025.
2. "Wanted – A Quality Education for All in Thailand." *World Bank Group*, n.d., worldbank.org. Accessed 8 Jan. 2025.
3. "Wanted – A Quality Education for All in Thailand."
4. Gary Buswell. "Human Rights in Thailand." *Expatica*, 15 Dec. 2024, expatica.com. Accessed 8 Jan. 2025.
5. Kelly Ng. "Thailand: 10 Million Sought Treatment for Pollution-Related Illnesses in 2023." *BBC*, 5 Mar. 2024, bbc.com. Accessed 8 Jan. 2025.
6. "NC 4: Global Boiling and Climate Change: Impacting Every Life across Thailand." *United Nations Development Programme*, 28 Apr. 2024, undp.org. Accessed 8 Jan. 2025.

INDEX

ABOUT THE **AUTHOR**

MARY BATES

Mary Bates, PhD, is a freelance writer who lives in Rhode Island. She has authored several nonfiction books for children, including titles on malaria, climate change, and superstitions. When she's not writing, she enjoys being in nature, reading, making science crafts, and spending time with her two cats.